This story reflects the challenges D.B. Turtle faced throughout life. Being a child that was not wanted made him determined to find his path and become something that no one thought he could achieve.

I dedicate this to the one person who gave me the strength to survive, smile and somehow rise above the challenges of our society. Also to the VA providers who help me through the darkness and to be unafraid to tell my story.

D.B. Turtle

THE SOUL OF AN UNWANTED CHILD

AUSTIN MACAULEY PUBLISHERS™

LONDON • CAMBRIDGE • NEW YORK • SHARJAH

Ordering Information
Quantity sales: Special discounts are available on quantity purchases by corporations, associations, and others. For details, contact the publisher at the address below.

Publisher's Cataloging-in-Publication data
Turtle, D.B.
The Soul of an Unwanted Child

ISBN 9798891551572 (Paperback)
ISBN 9798891551589 (ePub e-book)

Library of Congress Control Number: 2023924676

www.austinmacauley.com/us

First Published 2024
Austin Macauley Publishers LLC
40 Wall Street, 33rd Floor, Suite 3302
New York, NY 10005
USA

mail-usa@austinmacauley.com
+1 (646) 5125767

Preface

While I sit here looking at the screen, I begin to think about my life's journey and what brought me to this moment of sharing this viewpoint. Our society, nation, and generation have finally come to the crossroad, which is creating individual choices, which embody the beliefs of every race, creed, religion, and gender.

However, because of the societal norms, the clash of the individual has become the battlefield within each house, town, city, and state. The question lies within only one statement, "Who's choice is it." What has caused the divide of acceptance verse understanding? What gives the right of the few to make the choices of so many?

While you read this through the lens of someone who had to live with the choice of one, while being treated by the behavior of many, reflect on yourself image in the mirror and ask, "How do I accept myself and how do I treat others because of my acceptance?" Which is right, fair, and just for the soul of a child who had no choice or voice.

Chapter 1

While my birth was not like most, the path to my first breath began in this manner. It was the fall within the state of North Carolina eastern region. A young black girl whose choices had placed her in the position of having a child before she graduated from high school. In the late '60s this was not an acceptable thing to be occurring in a Baptist home of a sharecropper who was treated less than by those who owned the land on which his family was living and surviving on by mere scraps earned by the backs of the parents and children living in a farm shack sitting back in the woods.

The month was October, and the year was 1967. On the morning of the ninth of October, this young black girl experienced pain like many women much older and some younger than her prior. In a small hospital about twenty miles from the farmhouse where she lived, she was giving birth to a child which she did not want.

Birth the first breath is taken by this unwanted soul, let's journey back to the how this moment came to be. From the pictures around the farmhouse, she was a beautiful young black girl. Just sixteen years old. Just like manner teenagers, she was in love with the boy from down the road. Driven by lust and the desire to have the boy next door, she challenged the other girls in the community to win him over first.

I was never told when the relationship began; however, given the nature and relationship of the families involved, it would not be a stretch to imagine it happening while working on the farms and attending the same high school. Other siblings were intertwined with the thoughts of falling in love, and this young black girl and boy gave way to the possibility themselves.

While medicine would tell us that somewhere between December of 1966 and January of 1967, these two teenagers connected in the most intimate way that humans could. This act causes a chain reaction which led to my journey the moment that it was completed.

So, now that you have the time, it is unclear as to the place this happened or the actual day. However, I can tell you from the moment that I was conceived, the nourishment of my soul began. Now, as I take you on this journey, I want you to think about all of the things you have encountered and the children you have watched or raised yourself.

When you get to the end of my journey, I hope that you find yourself reflecting on who you are and how the decisions made for you, by you or the indirect decisions of others created the mental and emotional baggage that you now carry in every room, moment of your life.

Chapter 2

From the moment of conception, my soul was contaminated by the surrounding which I had no influence. How can this be, I was not born for more than eight months later. My biological mother had begun to feed me the angry, pain, and dysfunctional views from within herself. This was being done through the only existing lifeline that an unborn child has, the umbilical cord.

This pipeline is the key to an unborn survival, while some have written that it transfers the blood and nutrients necessary for life. I would add that it also transfers the pain, bitterness, hatred, and all other facets associated with the mindset of the mother. For me, this was the beginning of the erosion within the soul that was yet to be developed.

From everything I gathered about my biological parents, my mother and father should have never allowed me to be born. However, given the time and place, I would assume that was not an option. The mother, fear of rejection from a young man, afraid of the backlash from the family made the decision to carry this soul does not know the damage that she would impose on it by her own behaviors.

As I reflect, I often wondered what was going through her mind and how it feed into my soul. Did she lay awake at night feeling embarrassed, angry, outcast, and ashamed? When these thoughts we through her mind, how did this translate into a vile fluid that feed into the unborn child she carried.

Imagine being forced to digest this type of substances every day for more than eight months of your life. Imagine the erosion of the undeveloped structure as it develops into what appears to be a normal child. Having experienced the environment after birth, I can only imagine what it was like to be her. Having a father who was an alcoholic and a mother who believed in God as her lifeline for keeping a family together.

Living in a rural community in the south in the late sixties, a black unwedded pregnant girl, what kind of conversations were being had both with her and behind her back. She was growing up in a sharecropper's home which set off into the woods about twenty miles from the nearest town. In the house were ten other children, five boys and four other girls.

Over the course of the next eight months, did she try to hide this from the family? Or was this something the family was trying to hide from the community? While this is something that was never explained to me, I was fed the results of the decisions from all parties involved. Each day she awoke, she began to feed my soul through the lens in which she was being treated by those around her, both family and friends.

During this period, the biological father disappeared from the picture. While only miles away, it probably felt like being separated by the ocean or a greater distance. The question for me was, what was going through his mind?

How could he just walk away from this, knowing or unknowingly the impact on their decision to bring this child into the world? Just to give you an insight into the father, he was a black young man. His family lived on a farm; however, the land was owned by his father.

He also had ten brothers and sisters. But their economics was different than many others within the community. I was never told why he chose not to acknowledge me as his child, nor did I ever ask him. But I always wonder what the answer would have been if we could have had the conversation.

Now that I have given you a peek into the world in which this soul was created, let us focus on what happened to this unwanted soul. At time grew near to giving birth, I often wondered what was going through my mother's mind. Would she embrace me in a loving manner? Would she discard me as if I only took up space with no value?

It was a brisk October morning in 1967 when I entered this world. I was never told who was there to greet me, nor was I told that my biological mother received me. I was told, however, that I was taken to the place that I would call home and placed in a shoe box because I was so small that there was a fear of me dying if I slept in the same bed with someone else. Not knowing if this is true, I was also told that I was placed in a dresser drawer as my first bed.

Now that I no longer was digesting the vile from the body and mind of my biological mother. I was being fed the toxic oxygen from within the walls that I would now call home. Once at this place called home, at some point my biological mother made the decision that she would no longer want me in her life and left me with her mother. As time passed, I grew to know this person as my mom.

While I never called her mom, she would be referred to as grandma, and her husband would be called granddad. While I learned to crawl, walk, talk, and do all the things that a child should be doing. I also learned things that a child should never have to experience. My granddad was an alcoholic and would come home every night drunk. While he did not physically hit my grandmother, the verbal abuse in the home was enough to scare me for life.

I remember being five years old and watching my granddad get sick every night after dinner, throwing up his food, and passing out. He would wake up the next morning, start drinking, and do it all over again each night while cursing out my grandma. My granddad passed away when I was 6 years old at home. This event began to expose the emotional issues that would manifest themselves throughout my life.

I was getting off the bus from school when I saw a big black car in front of the house. I saw two men taking something out of the house which I later found out that it was my granddad's body. No one told me what was going on at the time. I remember the smell in the house, and I took off running and hid in the drainage pipe near the road. My heart pounding, sweating, and not knowing what to do, I sat there, hoping that someone would come get me. However, no one ever came, only the darkness, and I made my way back to the house without anyone acknowledging me.

After a few days had passed, we went to a church; and I saw his body in a box, and I walked away. My biological mother had returned for this a few days prior but did not talk to me or even hold me. She left a few days later without telling me where she would be. After the death of my granddad, things really got bad in the house.

My grandma's biological children treated me like an outsider and made fun of me every chance they got. I was the joke in the house as well as the maid. I was made to do all the things that no one else wanted to do or felt that I must do to earn my keep in the house. My grandma's kids were older than me by many years. She only had five left in the house at this time; the others had moved away along with my biological mother.

Her youngest son left in the house was the worst; he would pick on me every day and make me feel like I did not matter. The others would just use me to do things for them, such as wash their cars and clean the house. My grandma's youngest daughter had her first child when she was still in high school. I became the in-house babysitter once that happened. While other boys in the neighborhood were out playing and doing things, I was sitting home and changing diapers and learning how to cook and clean for other children.

By the time I was eleven years old and a lot of the damage was done, so I thought. As time passed, I would go to school, come home to take care of a newborn, and sit in the dark, wishing I could have fun like most kids in the community. No one ever asked about how school was going or even if I was passing my grade. I struggled with homework, but no assistance was given.

I struggled with my identity as I watched my aunts and uncles' behavior with drugs, alcohol, and relationships. Watching these things transpire continued the damage to my soul. This environment created images about relationships which I thought were normal. My aunts were having children and not married. My uncles were married but sleeping with other women at the same time. This made me think that my biological parents were just doing what was normal, except for leaving me as if I was a discarded penny.

I believe my grandma was trying to teach me thing and that was the reason for her taking me to church every Sunday. It seems like she wanted me to live my life based on the church rules; however, this created more conflict.

While my aunts and uncles had several children by different people, they seemed to always spend time and took care of them in their own way. Their children seemed happy because they were with their parents. Two of my aunts have boys near my age, and I wanted to be like them and have the things that they were given. One of my cousins was one year older, and the other one was the same age. One lived in North Carolina, about eight miles from my house; the other lived in New York with his parents.

Now as a teenage black unwanted child, the damage began to grow deeper into the soul. I watched my cousins enjoy the things a normal boy should be doing. The oldest would spend time with his father and mother. However, his father was having an affair with another woman, but it did not seem to bother his mother. They would carry on as if that were normal in a marriage and his sister who were older, put on the appearance of a perfect family for all to see.

The cousin who lived in New York had it all. His mother was the perfect "June Clever." The house was always clean, and everything was controlled with her children. Her on would walk around with all the name-brand clothing and money in his pocket. He would act like he was better than the rest of the kids in the family because he would get everything he asked for from his father and mother.

From the age of eleven to sixteen, my lens of a family and what happiness supposed to be shattered. The neighborhood was changing around me, and my environment was getting worse as each year passed. I was picked on about everything, from my size to the color of my skin, by both family and so-called friends and everyone in between. I withdrew within myself, which made things even worse.

As my body and mind changed, I was challenged about my sexuality and being afraid of sex. While all of this going on, I was still treated in the house like the butler and babysitter. There were times when all of the family would get together and I thought I would have fun; however, I was made to watch the kids while both of my cousins were allowed to hang out with the rest of the men and go places.

I would watch them drive off and laugh at me for sitting there with the younger children. The women would sit around and talk, and when one of the kids needed something, they would call me to do it or tell me to go play with them.

On my thirteenth birthdays, I remember I had a crush on the girl who lived down the road. She was beautiful, and I wanted to get to know her. I was so afraid to tell her because no one had ever told or taught me about anything when it came to dating. I watched her and made her laugh when I could, and she told me we were friends. To me, that was enough, because she did not treat me like I was less than.

When the summer came, I wanted to spend time with her and just have fun like other boys my age were during. However, I had to work on the farm now that I was older. I was shorter and smaller than my cousins, and I was not allowed to do a lot of things because of the way people saw me. When I started working on the farm, I earned money but was not allowed to keep it. I had to give it to my grandma because I was treated as if I did not know how to handle money, and no one had the time to teach me. I never saw the money and often wondered what happened to it, but was too scared to ask.

As the summer passed, I was picked on by my cousins because they all claimed to be having sex. I would wonder about sex, but none of my uncles ever talked to me about it. It was not talked about in school. Growing up in the Bible Belt, there were many things that were taboo, which made my environment so confusing.

I would listen to the adult conversation in and out of the house. The men would talk about women and sex while they drank and smoked. The women would talk about other women, call them names, and talk bad about their children because they had different fathers. I was confused because most of my aunts and uncles had children by different partners; however, they seemed to think they were better than others.

As the summer ended, I was afraid to go to school because I would be in high school. I feared being laughed at by the older boys. I did not want to be around other kids who wore name-brand clothes, and I wore things that were given to me or bought without thinking about what I liked or how they looked on me. Being unwanted meant not having a voice in the environment that you were placed in. I just had to take whatever came my way and appreciated the fact that I was allowed to be there.

I remember the first day of high school. As I stood waiting for the bus, I watched as the cars passed by. I remembered seeing a car that I had seen many times drive past the house; however, this morning my thoughts were somewhere else. I had overheard the women in the house talk about who my biological father was and that I saw him every day. The women also talked about his wife and children as if they were the blame for me not being in his life.

As the car approached, I noticed that it was the same car that was spoken about in the women's conversation. As it got close to me, I looked right at the driver as he drove past. He did not look at me; however, it felt as though I was looking in a mirror. Because during those conversations the women were having, it was also said that I was named after him and looked just like him.

As I watched the car disappear into the morning sun, other thoughts ran through my head. By this time, the bright yellow bus was stopped in front of me, and my heart started to pound as I took each step to climb up. While I knew most of the kids on the bus, it was painful to walk down the aisle, as in my mind everyone was talking about me and pointing at my clothes. I sat along on the ride and did not speak to anyone. I listen as the kids laughed and talked while I sank down in the seat to become invisible, just as I have felt my entire life.

Chapter 3

During my high school years, I experienced things that no child should have to in an environment where they are to be educated for their future success. Some of these emotional events took place at school, while others continued in the home. My grandma's youngest son was a senior at this high school when I started. He had a reputation for being a bully, and many other things. As I lurked in the shadows, trying not to draw attention to myself, I heard the voices in the hallways talking about me and while others pointed their fingers when I was near.

I also had a cousin who was one grade ahead of me at the high school. He was about he treated me about the best of anyone in the family. While he had his own friends, he tried to include me in things when he could or felt he had to, for reason I didn't know. The first semester was brutal; I was lost, and in a world of people who could have just discarded me like the wrapping from their snacks and I would not have been missed.

I was being picked on in every class that I attended, and the worst was gym. I would be left out of activities or made fun of when I tried to participate. Also made to feel like I was not young made when it came to my body. I was so ashamed of myself that I did not want to be around anyone, regardless of what was going on.

I became so with drawn that I began to act as if nothing bothered me and walked around with a smile on my face all the time. People began to think I was the happiest kid around, and some started to talk to me and even asked me to hang out with them.

This is when I realized that I had to put on a mask in this world if I wanted to survive. By the end of the semester, I had become the master of disguise. I could blend in with any group at any given time or in any situation. For the first time in my life, I felt good, even though it was fake. For the first time in high school, I had a young girl who wanted to spend time with me and talk. When my uncle and cousin saw this, they began to put the pressure on me to have sex. And this was the beginning of me losing control of my disguise. I did not know what to do; no one had ever talked to me about sex. I was completely lost, but also wanted everyone to continue to accept me under this disguise. I had to figure it out and fast. I did not want to lose the friendship that I was creating with this young girl, but I did not want to be treated like an outcast by the boys and men in my family.

The holiday break was coming up, and I thought this would be a good time to figure out a plan to keep my exterior mask intact. During the holiday break, I was able to spend time with one of the young girls in the neighborhood. While together, we explored each other's bodies but never had sex. I felt this was a step in the right direction for me to be accepted by individuals of my own gender. During the remainder of the holiday break, I was brought back to reality by the way I was treated by those who were supposed to love me and those who called me part of the family.

During the Christmas time, my biological family got together for a big celebration at my grandma's house. They would decorate the tree, put lights up, and cook all kind of foods. All of my aunts and uncles would come back from all over the east coast. This is when the belittling would begin. As soon as their children walked into the house, I would begin to be treated as if I did not exist. Well apart from taking care of the small children that now invaded the space I thought was my home.

The cousins that were my age were allowed to go to town, hang out with the adults, and go to other places while I was left behind to attend to the children's needs or play butler to the adults that were around the house. I would try and find a place to hide so that I did not have to do all of the chores, but more so to not feel as though I was not worthy of anyone's love, attention, or value in any way.

I wanted Christmas to be over quickly; at least then I could get back into an environment that I had trained myself to survive in. Christmas day arrived, and the emotional torment would continue as I watched all of my cousins get gift after gift. But the torment came from my own biological mother, who at this time had two children with her husband, and they were with her. She had given them all of the things they wanted for Christmas, and for me, she gave me things that had no connection to me at all.

She never asked me what I liked or wanted. She would just buy random things and give them to me, and family members would look at me as if I was some stranger getting a handout from the family. I hated every moment of

Christmas because it made me feel like I was a second thought to everyone around me. No one in the room cared about how I was feeling or wanted to know. I was just a body taking up space in the house, and I should appreciate being given the opportunity to breathe in their space.

After gifts were opened at my grandma's house, I was then transported to my father's biological parents house to do it all over again. This made the day even more tragedy because now I was placed in an environment out of pity and not love. When family takes you places out of what they consider obligation and not out of love, in their minds they are doing the right thing. However, they have no idea how this is impacting the child being carried around like a piece of luggage or object that needs to be placed on display.

Each year that this occurs causes me to withdraw from anyone and everyone in the family. Regardless of the intent being made to feel like I was on display as the bastard child for all to look at examine was one of the most painful things I ever experienced at this point in my life. Sitting in that room, I felt as though everyone was judging me based on every aspect that the human eye could visually process. I could feel the pity from their own words and actions. The most painful thing to endure was to watch once again the man who was part of my creation discard me as if I was less worthy of his name, let alone his DNA.

Just as my biological mother had done time and time again, he sat there, not looking at me, while the children from his marriage were showed with love and gifts from all those within the family and himself. By the end of the night, I was emotionally exhausted and just wanted to go and hide from the world surrounding me. I was loaded back into the car like cargo for transport and taken to the place that I called home. Which at this point, the environment mirrored what I just experienced.

After finding a place to lay down because I did not have my own room in this house. I lay there staring at the ceiling with tears in my eyes. I could hear others in the house talk about the day. My biological mother's voice was in the background with the other women. They judged what happened throughout the day, and some even mentioned my name. However, that only lasted for a moment, and then they spoke about all the good things that were going on with their kids.

I remember hearing my biological mother talk about her other two sons and how they were doing so good in sports and wanted to give them all the things they needed for school. As I drifted off to sleep, the tears grew and the pain deepened. The year I turned thirteen was the year that I knew I was not like the rest of the family in the house that I called home. I was now at an age where I was able to evaluate this environment for what it really was. This was not a home for me; it was a place that I had been put in because of the shame and beliefs of individuals.

This house was a crate meant to hold me until I outgrew it. It was not a place meant to provide love, support, or protect me from the world. I was just like any other tool purchased for this farm; my purpose was to be used in a manner needed at the time to fulfill the needs of others. For the family living here, the downfall with me was the cost associated with keeping this bastard around. I was a living breathing tool, which required someone to give me nourishment to ensure I could do the work needed.

Chapter 4

This nourishment needed came with a price; someone had to invest their time, energy, and money into this unwanted soul or tool, depending on who was giving up these items to me. Now in high school and starting to truly process who I was and how I was being treated by those who were referred to as my family. I began to internalize everything around me. I did not or would not allow anyone to get to know me. I smile around everyone, making them believe that I was the quiet kid who never got into trouble and everyone could trust.

Meanwhile, inside of my mind and body, I was the small boy who was eroding from the absence of love, acceptance, and understanding from all of them. I put on the show that was needed to survive around all of them when needed. When I was with my male cousin, I talked about sex and did the things that they were doing with and to girls. When I was around the house, I did everything I was told to do by everyone who was older than me.

There were times when I pushed back like most teenagers, and that's when I would get the beatings from my grandma with a switch or belt. I would get a lot of beatings from the age of thirteen until I was around sixteen. Many times, I was just acting out my emotions from within, and it came out as being rebellious, or sometimes I would not want to do what I was being told because I was tired of being the "house boy" for everyone else. So, I would just take the beating and then end up being made to do the chores anyway.

What was one more beating for being the bastard, just another day in the life of this unwanted soul? Over the next three years, I learned how to survive even better, which gave me the ability to maneuver in the house and around the family successfully. I remember one of my uncles and his wife stopped by the house in North Carolina on their way to the beach for vacation with their daughter. I was told they wanted me to go with them. This was exciting to me because I have never been taking on a vacation. While on the outside I was excited, inside I was wondering just what this little journey was going to cost me.

I went on the trip and, for a moment, allowed myself to enjoy the beach and the things that were being given to me. When we returned to North Carolina, reality set in. The car stopped in front of the house, and I got out. The moment that I entered the house, I was the "house boy" once again. The smile on my face lasted for a short moment as I started to do the chores, I had allowed myself to think that maybe there was a chance I was going to be like the other boys my age.

When I turned sixteen, I wanted to get my driver's license and get a car, like most young men that age. My grandma worked it out that I could use her sister's car to take the test, and I was excited. None of my uncles or aunts took the time to teach me to drive. I took the course through the school and was determined to get my license so I could get out of this crate called home. On the day I went to get my driver's license, I passed the test, and when I walked out of the station in town, I saw something amazing.

I was looking at twenty state patrol officers and their cars all in a row. I had no idea about what they did or anything, but at the moment I saw everyone around me move out of their way and treat them as if they were gods. At that moment, I said to myself, I will wear that uniform so that I can be respected like that someday. I never told anyone about that moment, partly because they probably would have made fun of me. but mostly because my family history with the police.

I left that station with a dream, and I thought no one could take that away from me. Now that I got my driver's license, I thought maybe my uncles would treat me more like an adult than the little boy no one wanted around. However, that did not change; it got worse. I remember my uncle letting me drive his car with a friend of his because they had been drinking. While driving along, my uncle had told his friend to pretend to put a gun in my side and tell me to drive the car faster. They both thought this would be funny. I was so afraid that I was driving more than ninety miles per hour, and at one point, just wanted to drive straight into a tree and get it over with.

Finally, they both started yelling for me to slow down while they laughed. When we got back to the house, I jumped out of the car and never looked back. I left the house for the next few hours and walked into the woods. I sat near a tree and thought about what they would tell all their friends and the rest of the men in the family about how I acted while they laughed at me. I was always the butt of everyone's jokes.

Christmas was coming around again, and I was not in the mood to deal with the shit that had occurred over the years that I could remember. This Christmas, I wanted to be different, I took a bold step and asked my biological mother for a specific gift. My cousin, who was a year older than me, had gotten a car from his father earlier in the year. Even though his father and mom were separated from each other because his dad was sleeping around with other women, his dad still treated him like his son.

I asked my biological mother to buy me a car for Christmas, and she laughed at me. They all laughed at me when she told them. I told her I wanted to get a job, and I would pay her back. She told me she would not put her money into something like that for me. Just for a moment, I thought I was finally at the age where I could be treated with some respect. This moment took me back in time and re-enforced what I have always felt, abandon and discarded with no value to anyone. Even my grandma, who I thought was my saver, spoke out about this, but not in my favor.

This was the last Christmas in which I ever asked or expected to get anything from anyone in this family, even again. My soul was discarded and now deepened with disconnection from them all. My survival skills had been heightened over the last few years, and now I had to put everything that I had learned into play to make it out of this crate, which I had been placing in by those who presented themselves as caring, loving individuals throughout the family and the community.

This was the year that was closer for me. I was forced to change schools by state law. I had to get up at 5 a.m. to get to a school that did not want me there as a black kid. I had to learn now to assimilate in this environment to survive and move on from another moment of being treated less than by those around me. My last couple of years of high school solidified the foundation which created my lens for the next ten years of my life. I became a true master of disguise by being in an environment of racial differences and biases from all angles of life.

I kept my head down and moved within the shadows of the school grounds and the shadows within the family unit. I became the unnoticeable individual in the room. While they saw my smile, they never asked about my feeling, my needs, or what I wanted. To them, in their lens, I was that unwanted soul that they could not get away from because of the stain it would place on themselves. I blended into my surroundings like a chameleon in the jungle; self-preservation was the only goal to achieve.

I never really had a relationship while in high school, not from the lack of trying. I found myself in a space of girls liking me for the perception that I portrayed but did not want to be with me because of the judgment that followed. My view of a healthy relationship was something that would cause problems for me in the future, but for now I had to play the game. My first sexual experience was in high school at the school. It was with a young girl whom I knew but had no relationship with. It was more of a rite of passage and to keep the vultures at bay, i.e., bullies and members of my family, from looking at me if I was sexually challenged in some way. I won't go into details; however, it took place in a room where most boys should not have been. My first orgasm was exciting and terrifying at the same time. When it was over, she got dressed, smiled, and walked away. I stood there for a moment, not knowing what to say or do, so I got dressed and walked away, wondering, was that it? Would I now be accepted into the club? Would my cousins and uncles and the guys in the neighborhood finally stop teasing me? Well, the answer to that was no.

It seems like once you are in the club, you now have to continue to conquer other girls to validate your status. While my sexuality was never questioned, I had sex with girls that I had no connections to over the next two years as a way to mentally and physically cope with the environment surrounding me.

My senior year finally arrived, and I could see the light at the end of the tunnel. So, I began to plan my escape from this crate, which I had been placed in for almost eighteen years. I did not know what I was going to do; however, I knew I needed to get as far away from this toxic environment and fast. During my senior year, I watched as my uncles were arrested for numerous things, from drunk driving to drugs. I watched my aunts have more babies by other men, and all I could think about was being trapped there to take care of them.

The hardest part of planning my escape was not telling my grandma about the plan. I did not want to take the change of her trying to keep me there, nor did I want her to know how unhappy I was. She had tried to provide me with a place to grow up in the only way she could. I could not blame her for this; she took this unwanted soul into her home.

The first semester was coming to an end, and I was still trying to figure out where to run. No one in the family gave me guidance on anything. No one talked about me getting a job or going to college. It was like it had been for the entire span of my life. I had been existing without existing. I was not worthy of their efforts, and this bastard had served its purpose within the crate.

I applied to a couple of colleges and got accepted; however, no explained the process to me. The school counselors were more concerned with the white students and less concerned about some little poor black kid that no one even knew his name. I was not aware of anyone in the family going to college, nor did anyone talk about it, so I let that possibility dissipate. I took the military entrance exam as my next option. My scores came back high, and I was contacted by several recruiters. After meeting with them all, I decided to join the Air Force. I went to the MEPS center, passed all of the requirements, and enlisted right away. Now I felt like I had a plan, and no one in the family could stop me from doing what I wanted to do. I did not tell anyone in the family about my leaving.

When I graduated from high school, the family tradition was to have a party. Just like all of the things in my life, it was a façade, and I played along so that they could get drunk and pat each other on the back. I left North Carolina after graduating and went to spend my last summer in New York, staying at an aunt's house. I got a job working in a warehouse so that I did not have to depend on anyone giving me anything. I had been made to feel like I owed everyone something for being allowed to grow up in their space.

As the summer came to an end, I knew it was only a matter of months before I was gone, and I would never come back to this place again. I counted the days once I got back to North Carolina, and the days did not go by fast enough.

On my eighteenth birthday, everyone was asking me what I was going to do. Did I have a job because I could not live in the house anymore. That night I told them all I was leaving, and they did not have to worry about me anymore. I left them with that in their heads, trying to figure out what I meant by that. I was in the last thirty days before I left for Lackland Air Force Base in Texas. I was scared for many reasons; I had never been on a plane, nor had I ever been to Texas. Most of all, I was going to be in a place with strangers and did not know how I would be treated.

Even though I had all these fears, what could be worse than what I had already been exposed to by the people who called me family? I had been called everything from boy, bastard, cry baby, pussy, nigger, and most hurtful unwanted by those who also said they loved me when others were around. But never to my face. So, to have strangers say these things was like no big deal. I want you to find me, who I could be, and who I wanted to be.

I left home the day of November 25, 1985, and never looked back. I hugged my grandma and thanked her for all that she had done. While I carried a lot of scars with me, she had done her best and done more than most. As I sat in the airport waiting to leave, I stared out of the window, wondering what was awaiting me when I landed. Once on board the plane, I buckled up and looked straight ahead. As the plane taxied for takeoff, my stomach dropped, and when

I felt it off the ground, I almost threw up. After about an hour, I was feeling better, and the lady walking down the aisle said we would be in San Antonio in about three hours, I began to breathe differently.

When the plane landed, I was met by Air Force personnel along with a large group of other people all going to basic training. We were loaded into big buses and driven to Lackland Air Force Base. Upon our arrival, people were yelling and screaming and throwing things around. I thought to myself, *They can't break me no matter what they do.* At that moment, it started to rain as we started marching to the barracks for this journey to begin.

Chapter 5

Once at the barracks, all my things, which was much was being thrown around like they had no value. In retrospect, none of the items I had with me had no value whatsoever. Once the yelling stopped and everyone was standing in front of their beds, we were told to get some sleep. I laid my head down on the pillow and thought to myself, *I am searching for who I supposed to be at this moment in my life.*

What seemed life only moments had passed, the yelling began again, this time it was only four forty-five in the morning. As we rushed down the stairs, almost falling over each other, the instructor continued to yell as loud as he could. We stood in line, which later was known as formation. I looked straight ahead while watching the individuals to my left and right shake with fear. I could not understand why I was not shaking like others around me, but then it hit me like a brick. This was the only way I knew how to be treated; for the others, maybe it was the first time they were made to feel less than and did not know how to process this environment.

This was the first day of many more like this to come. Each day for the next eight weeks, I faded into the background, kept my head low, and did not draw attention to myself. My survival skills had kicked in, and time seemed to fly by. Some of my teammates weren't so lucky. One night, while on fire watch, I found a young man climbing out of the window. I was supposed to sound the alarm, yet I watched as he crossed the window seal and out of my view. Moments later, everyone was up, and people were yelling and running around.

I stood there at attention, telling the sergeant what I saw. By the afternoon, we all learned that the individual was OK, but would not be joining the team anymore. I watched how people on the team acted after getting the news. Some individuals cried, while others just whispered in the corners with those who they began friendships with. I sat alone and thought to myself, *What was so bad that made him want to hurt himself?*

For me, this place was magical; I was treated just like everyone else regardless of my differences, and while I got singled out sometimes, so did everyone else. I began to focus on what was next for me. First, survive basic training, then off to my school for my job. However, I had no idea what I wanted to do, but I knew within the next week I would have to make a choice. After a couple of days in the field learning how to read maps, set up tents, and other tasks, I found myself in an office with a Staff Sergeant to talk about what I wanted out of my career.

Sitting here and hearing words like my career and what I wanted to do was like listening to a foreign language being spoken. No one in my life until now ever asked me what I wanted or what was important to me. After about ten minutes or so, the Sergeant put a list of jobs in front of me and said, *Nice scores, these are the jobs you can be trained on after the completion of basic training.* I can only remember a few of them: Security Police, Personnel and Weapons Technician. I had no idea what I could or could not do. I had not really applied myself in school, nor did I truly understand the score the Sergeant was talking about.

Until this point, I had not talked to anyone about being in the military or how to decide what I wanted to do. The only thing kept coming to my mind was the day I saw the State Troopers in their uniforms, so I decided right then to become a Military Police Officer. How could I go wrong with wanting to help others and enforce the law? When I told the Sergeant what I had chosen, the Sergeant said, "I am surprised with the scores you got" but hey, someone must do it. The Sergeant completed some paperwork and told me to congrat and send in the next airman.

I walked away with a smile, not knowing exactly what all of this meant; however, it was something I got to choose, and for the first time, I felt as though I was in control of my life. Now it was up to me to make it or not, and I could not blame anyone else for this choice. That night, I laid in my bunk thinking about everything I left behind. I was scared, alone, and had no one I could trust with my feelings, so I began to build the vault inside my mind and body to lock all of the things away that I was afraid or ashamed of to protect myself from any more emotional pain.

As the weeks passed, and graduation came closer, I was outperforming many of the people on my team. I was so focused on completing this that it did not matter about the pain or being tired; I could not fail because it would mean that all of them were right about me in their eyes. For the first eighteen years of my life, all I heard from the people who claimed they loved me and cared for me was that, I was the bastard child and that I would be lucky to do anything with my life. The only thing I was good at was taking care of other people's children. I was too small to amount to anything and to settle for any job I could get.

This became the fuel to push me through the pain, failure, and anything else they tried to do to me during basic. I had enough fuel to last me a lifetime, and no one was going to stop me from making through this process and much more. The graduation day arrived, I sat on my bed in my dress uniform watching my teammates talk about their families coming to see them march across the parade grounds. The excitement of watching them refueled my desire to succeed, knowing that at the end of this day I would be standing alone once again with no one there to say "congrats or I am proud of you," no father or mother to take photos with, nor a brother or sister to share the moment with.

While experiencing one of the greatest accomplishments in my life, I felt as though I stood in the shadow of everyone around me. Just as I had felt all my life in the house that I grew up in, never acknowledged in a positive way for anything I did, nor treated as if I existed many days when I woke up. There I stood in my dress blue uniform, surrounded by people that I had only known for eight weeks, but felt closer to them than I had felt to anyone in my life. When the celebration was over, I grabbed my gear that was packed the night before to head off to my school for the job that I had chosen.

The next leg of my journey was not far. I did not have to get on a plane like many of my classmates. I walked across the base for about 2 miles and arrived at my next place for training. Just like before, upon my arrival, I was greeted in the military fashion. My lead instructor called out a list of names and room numbers and stated, "Put your shit away and settle in until Monday morning, when classes began." As I walked down the hallway to my assigned room, I wondered who my next roommate would be. When I arrived and opened the door, on one of the beds was a white guy sleeping.

I took my gear, placed it in the locker provided, and laid it across my bed. As I laid there, my mind went through all the things that I had been running from. I thought about my grandma and whether or not she was proud of me. I thought about all the pain I felt inside from being abandoned by the two people who brought me into this world. Then I felt tears running down the side of my face. I rolled over, wiped my face, and told myself to never cry again.

For the next forty-eight hours, I prepared myself for what was to come. I had become a master of leaving things in the past and moving forward. While I did not want to forget some of my teammates from basic training, I knew that I would need to let them go, keep my emotions hidden, and protect myself from the pain and teasing that was about to come over the next ten weeks.

I told myself no one in this school could treat me any less than what I had already experienced as a child. Therefore, I was prepared to complete any task given and never let them break me at no cost. Over the next ten weeks, I was pushed beyond anything that I had experienced physically. I was tired, body was aching, and I began to doubt myself once again. I remember about week number eight, and we were performing field training at night. I was sitting alone in a foxhole doing security; it was pitch black, and I could not see anything. As my mind wondered, I told myself that I could not allow anyone to break me and that I had no choice but to finish this to prove them all wrong about me.

This was the moment of truth and the energy that I needed to get me over the hump. When the field exercise was completed, it was all downhill. We began to out process and get our assignments, and my heart was beating as fast as it had ever before. As they called out the names and the assignments, I watched the reactions of my classmates. Some of them were happy, and some sad because they were not going to be close to home. For me, I was hoping to get as far away as possible. I did not care where they were sending me, as long as it was not back to North Carolina.

When they called my name, I answered, and my instructor stated, "California." I jumped up with the biggest smile on my face. My roommate was from California, and he had told me so much about it. Unfortunately, he got Minot, North Dakota, and was not happy. He asked me to trade with him, and I told him sorry, but this was my chance to see California, and I could not pass it up. As we walked away from getting our assignments, I could not stop smiling and thinking about being three thousand miles from the place I called home, which was more like a place of pain for me.

The next two weeks flew by, and I was on a plane to California. I did not take any leave, as many of my classmates did prior to their first assignment. I wanted nothing more than to forget about that place and begin my own life, and make my own decisions. When I arrived, it was like heaven. The sun was shining, and the sky was as bright as a light. I took a taxi for the first time to the main gate of the base and showed them my orders. I arrived at my squadron and reported in.

Scared, but excited, I could not sleep. I had to take days off before reporting for duty. As I walked around the barracks, learning where things were, some people spoke to me while others just went about their business. Later that Sunday night, my roommate returned to the barracks and opened the door. He was surprised that I was there but greeted me and told me to relax; it would get better. He had been in one year longer than me and had earned two stripes. I was a slick sleeve, and as far as that went, I was at the bottom when it came to duty assignments and details.

My first official day arrived, and I reported to my Flight Sergeant. He told me to relax and introduced me to the team. Then I met my Lt., who was a female, very tall and thin. I was assigned to a Staff Sergeant's team and was told that he would be responsible for my training and work assignments.

After being shown around the squadron and taken out of my post, my squad leader told me that he would be back and left me there with my weapon and instructions. I was so excited and nervous at the same time. I did not want to make a mistake, so I stood there, focused on everything going on around me, and never left my post. As security, we had a code that we conducted our duties by that did not apply to any others on the air base. I learned those codes and did everything I could to make sure I not only knew my duties but was the best at them.

I was assigned to all the areas through the base as part of my training because I had to pass my certification within the first six months of my assignment. I studied like crazy, and when it was time, I passed with flying colors. My team leader told me that if I had failed, he would have recommended me to be discharged from the Air Force. Now his true color was coming out, and he was a prick. He began to treat me like I was less than him, not because of his rank but just because he felt he was better.

This motivated me to learn everything I could without telling him what I knew. I wanted to make sure that he could not put me in a place that I could fail to prove that I did not belong. I was excelling as I got my first stripe and then my second one. Now I was not the new guy who did not know anything. Things were going great, and then one day I was called into the OP's officer's office. I was scared because I had never been called into the admin office before. When I arrived, the captain was sitting behind his desk with papers in front of him. I reported, saluted, and stood at attention.

The captain said, "At ease," I relaxed as much as we were allowed to, and he stated that you must be excited. I could not understand why he would make a statement like that. He stated that I was being reassigned to Belgium but had to go to a school first. He handed me my orders and stated good luck. I saluted and left the office. On the way back to my post, my team leader said, "You luck fuck." I been trying to get orders out of here for a while, and you get them within your first year.

I did not know what this all meant. I got back to my room and read the orders, which stated I was beginning to be assigned to Belgium and going to school in Arizona prior to my assignment. I did not even know where Belgium was and had to look it up on the map. When I discovered that it was in Europe and near France and Germany, I was excited. This was another thing that no one in my dysfunctional family had experienced, and I was going to see the world and more.

As I packed the things I had bought and all of my gear, I could not stop thinking about being able to travel and see the United States and now going to see Europe. The next three months flew by, and I was on my way to Arizona for training. The school was ten weeks old, and it was hell all over again. I was being trained to guard resources that many people did not even know about. I was told that I could not discuss anything with anyone. For me, this was easy because there was no one to talk to in my case. I focused on the school and the training and completed it successfully. When I finished the class, I was told I had to take a week of leave minimum before traveling over to Belgium.

While the rest of the Airmen were excited to go home, I was hoping I could just get on a plane and never look back. However, I got on a plane and flew back to North Carolina. I had to contact my cousin to have them pick me up from the airport. When I arrived, everyone was looking at me like I was from another planet. Some asked me about what had been going on, while others just wanted to know what I was doing with my money and then asked for it. My grandma was in the house, and she gave me a big hug, and she started to cry.

After everyone was gone, we sat and talked. I told her about some of the stuff, and she asked if I was OK. She told me she was proud of me; that was the first time anyone had ever acknowledged anything that I had done in my life. She told me to believe in myself and never let anyone tell you that you can't do something. This was not the grandma that I remembered; she was talking to me like I was an adult. She spoke to me like I mattered.

After about four days, I left North Carolina and went to New York to stay with my aunt because that is where I had to fly out of to get to Belgium. While in New York, it was back to the same shit that I had left. Everyone treated me like I was the little kid that they could just force me to do things. However, this time I pushed back, and they did not like it. I told them I would get a hotel room, and they could just forget me. My aunt told me to watch my mouth, so I just went into a room and stayed there until it was time for me to leave.

My biological mother lived a few miles away from where I was, but she never came to talk. Even on the day that I left, she did not even say anything. She had her other two sons with her, and they were the only thing that mattered to her.

When I got out of the car at the airport, I never looked back and just kept walking. There was nothing left for me in New York, just like nothing left for me in North Carolina. I was closing the chapters of both places in my life forever. I looked out of the window at the airplane, and I thought to myself, *This is my freedom bird, and I was ready to be free from all of the bullshit that I had been dealt in my life.*

Chapter 6

The flight was eight hours long. I had never been on a plane over the ocean, and my mind was playing tricks on me. I could not sleep, so I looked around in the low lite plane at the other passengers. I thought about who they were, where they were going, and if there were others on the plane like me. I saw others with military haircuts but was not sure.

I kept thinking about what my grandma told me before I left. Why did she say that? What did she mean by never left someone tell you, you can't do something? I also thought about the moment that she said she was proud of me. What caused her to tell me that now? Maybe I was trying to find something to hold onto because I had told myself I would never return to that place, no matter what.

What seemed like a day, the eight hours were over, and the plane was landing? When I got off the plane and walked through the airport, I began to tense up. There were police walking around with big weapons and people everywhere, and the language being spoke, I could not understand. I could not read the signs and began to panic. When I turned the corner, I spotted another American Soldier walking, and I just followed him. I had no idea where I was going, but I was not going to let him out of my sight. Then I spotted it, the USO, where I was supposed to report to and wait.

I walked a straight line right to the USO, reported in, and was told the bus would be leaving in two hours. I put my bags down, looked around, and asked the lady at the desk where to get something to eat. She told me where to go, and I headed out. Standing in line, I looked around at the people, and I could not believe I was in a foreign country. My eyes and mind could not process everything around me; it was overwhelming.

The bus arrived, and I got on it with about twenty-five others, and our journey began to the base where I would spend the next year of my life. Excited yet scared, for the first time in my life, I felt like I was doing something for myself that no one could every takeaway or make me feel like I owed them something. The drive was amazing; everything was so different, and all I could think about was making it on my own.

When we arrived at the base, I got my gear and was met by my supervisor. He took me to the barracks to drop off the gear, then right to the orderly room to report to the First Sergeant. I stooped there, shaking, and looked straight ahead when the First Sergeant arrived. He told me to relax and asked me some questions. After about ten minutes, he introduced me to my Flight Sergeant, and we left the building and talked as we walked toward another building where we would report for duty.

I was given the day to unpack and get squared away. I had to report to work the next morning to begin my training with my team. I unpacked and walked around to figure things out. Got some chow and a haircut. I sat near the barracks and watched the people coming and going until it started to rain. Finally, my roommate arrived and told me to come with him. I followed him into the neighbor's room, where there were about six people in there. They all introduced themselves and welcomed me. They gave me a beer and said welcome to the team. At first, I paused because I thought I was not old enough to drink, but then I realized that I was not in the United States and I could drink without getting into trouble.

I took a drink of the beer and started to relax and talk to the guys in the room. After a couple of beers, everyone went their own way, and I went back to my room and laid down. I was not a big drinker, and after being up for so long, I was tired and needed to get some sleep before work the next day. I fell asleep and did not wake up until the next morning, took a shower and got ready for work. This was the easy part; I did not have to think about what to wear or where to go; it was all planned out for me. My role was to be on time and to follow orders.

It took about a month for me to get into the swing of things, and I became one of the guys on the team. I began to work hard, workout, and drink a lot with the guys and my roommate. This became the daily routine because we did not have a lot to do on base and our time off was not so flexible. However, I did begin to go into town as much as I could to see the people and try the food, which I loved.

The people in this country were great, friendly, and enjoyed life to its fullest. After a couple of months, I met a local girl, and we started to hang out and travel together. She showed me the local sites and even travel to a couple of other countries together. She was beautiful, and I loved being around her. She would try to teach me the language, and her family treated me like I was one of them. I would stay at her house on the weekend sometimes when I did not have to work, and I felt happy for the first time in my life.

While I did not understand what a real relationship was, I tried to emulate the things I saw others doing in hopes that it was the right thing to do. Unfortunately, the role models for relationships in my life up to this point were not the best, nor did I have anything to measure success by. I watched both men and women who were married, but their spouses were back home, sleeping with as many people as they could. I was trying to understand the process of calling yourself married while having sex with other people without any hesitation.

I was told by several people that I started hanging out with that this is what happens when you are apart and that whatever happens here stays here, and you never take it back to your family. Having watched people in the house that I grew up in do the same things while at home, I thought this was the way a relationship was supposed to be like. While I began to have a strong feeling for the young lady that I met in town, I also started to have sex with other women on the base like everyone else was doing.

With the lack of experience in having sex with different partners and balancing the lies needed to maintain different relationships, I soon found myself feeling pain from losing the one girl that I really cared for. We met in town as usual, and while we were out, she started asking me if I was with other people. I did not know how to respond to this. Was I supposed to tell her the truth because everyone was doing it and I thought she was as well? Was I supposed to lie, tell her no, and keep trying to live two separate lives? Not having a true north to point toward, I told her the truth, and she started crying and did not want to see me anymore.

I was confused and hurt because I thought I was doing the right thing by being honest. After that night, I stayed on base for the next few weeks, sad and not wanting to be around anyone. I thought they would all know what happened and make fun of me like others had done throughout my life. After a few weeks of drinking and not going anywhere, my roommate told me to grow up and let it go. He told me that women are just like me; they want to have sex and play the relationship card when it's convenient for them. Then he said, *So get up and go find someone else to fuck and let it go.*

Going through this made me withdraw from most people because I did not want to feel hurt again. I wanted to feel loved and to love someone in return; however, I did not know how. Everything that I had been running from began to resurface, like the aching of joints from an injury. Each breath that I took felt like being back in the house, where I was invisible to everyone around me. Not knowing how to love caused me to believe that I could not be loved.

As my journey continued in this foreign land, so did my disconnect with my ability to love anyone. I met so many people who seemed to care about me; however, my mind and heart would not allow me to accept or trust that it was real. I played defense with the understanding that these individuals were only doing this to ensure they could come back and have leverage on me at some point in my life.

While I mastered the ability to not allow anyone into my heart, I also mastered the ability to portray the happy individual that everyone wanted to hang out with. The energy that it took to hide in plain sight was exhausting, both mentally and physically. As a child, I was taught to smile and be polite and knowing your place when you are around others. This played right into the culture of the military because rank had its privileges, and knowing your place helped you move through the organization better with fewer challenges from those above you.

I became very good at my duties and was rewarded for my performance and military bearing. Little did they know, I was just being the unwanted soul in the space I now occupy. I began to drink more, and more using it as a tool to help me keep down the sadness and the detachment from the space surrounding me. As I learned more of the lingo of military life, this assignment was referred to as a remote tour. For me, this was like survival training because of the restricted ability placed on me and no being able to run from things. I honed my skills at masking and assimilation of who I was, with the understanding of how to be accepted by those around me.

When my orders were up, I was notified that I was being reassigned back state side and my anxiety started to rebuild. I did not want to go home; I wanted to be as far away from those others would call family. I knew when I arrived back, there would be no one to greet me, no party, and no hugs. Once I knew where I was going stateside, I began to smile because my assignment was more than fifteen hundred miles away from the place that had created a soul of unacceptance.

I arrived back in the states and took the minimum amount of leave before going to my new base. I smiled and pretended that I was excited to see everyone, and they pretended to care about me being in the place called home. After a few days, it was back to normal, as if I was still the little boy that no one wanted. I packed my things and left without saying goodbye to more than half of them. I was on the run again, but this time I had better survival skills and was ready for the challenge.

It had been more than three years now since I started running. When I arrived at my new base, I was ready for the process this time. I knew what to do, who to see, and how it was going to work. Within a couple of days, I was settled in, and things were moving forward. My leaders did not need to train me as much because I had three years under my belt. I was a squared away Airman, and my Flight Sergeant was happy that I could carry my own without being told what to do each moment of the day. I was coming to the end of my enlistment and did not know what I was going to do. I was about to turn twenty-one, which meant I could start drinking again legally.

It was the summer, and I was beginning to feel good about my new surroundings. The cycle had begun: drinking, sex, and working, with working out in between. This was the life of the military as I knew it. I had no intentions of going to school at the time, and no one pushed me, with the exceptions of the schools, for my job in the military. As the first winter passed, I began to enjoy my new home. I became more proficient at my job and knowledge of the military, and began a competitor in things on the base. For a moment, I thought I had finally found a place that I could start learning who I was or could be. People did not treat me less than, nor did they make comments about my size, color, or ask about my parents. Which made things much easier for me because they only wanted to know me. However, no I realize those things are a part of me that I can never change.

I got orders again to go back overseas, and I was excited. I did not want to be in the states because I felt too close to the pain, and it began to consume me. Prior to going overseas, I had to attend a school for training for my new assignment. This placed me back into the mindset of survival again because schools were the hardest thing for me. I had never been supported or knew just how smart I was due to the lack of feedback from the "family." I left the base and headed to the school, which was located on the east coast, only a couple hundred miles from the place called home. I did not tell anyone that I would be there because I did not need the drama.

Upon my arrival, I settled into my room and met some of my classmates. By now, I had enough time in the military to be more relaxed because of my stripes and experience. This was a different environment given the fact that I was in the Air Force, and this was an Army post. I watched all of the new Airmen walk into the barracks, and I thought to myself, I remember those days. Looking like I was lost and not sure of anything. Then I notice a group of girls walking together, laughing and talking.

While I was focused on getting through the class and moving on, I also became attracted to one of the girls I saw the first day. We started to hang out and talk and get to know each other. This was a training base, so things were more restricted than being on a permanent assignment. Regardless, we hung out and had some fun. Over the next eight weeks, we walked, talked, and began to have sex when we could. This became a distraction for me with the drama that had been looming about the family. I was drinking very heavily at the time and just wanted to get on the freedom bird to my duty station overseas and leave all of this crap behind.

51

Chapter 7

At the end of the school, we talked about where we were headed and said our goodbyes. Again, I found myself wanting more but not knowing what a true relationship was. I just watched her leave, and I walked away. I was back at my base within the next twenty-four hours and found myself sitting alone in my room with a bottle of alcohol. I had four months before out processing and I was free from all the bullshit once again.

Having just re-enlisted so that I could go back overseas, I had six more years to serve, and I wanted to get started. It was only two days after the school that I found myself drunk and calling the girl that I had been with at the school. I told her to come visit me and let's have some fun. I sent her a plane ticket and a ring and told her if she did not come, she could still keep the ring. Then I thought to myself, *What are you doing? You don't know this girl, and you are not ready to get married.*

While all of that is true, I also don't want to be alone right now. Then I thought what I had to lose, a couple hundred bucks, I drink that much in a week. The day had come, and I got a call to pick her up from the airport. I drove two hours away to get her, and we talked more on the ride back to the base. She was pretty, funny, and free-spirited. We party with the guys I worked with and made plans to get married at the courthouse before she left for her permanent assignment. This was probably the most random thing I had done in my life, but there was nothing or no one I had to confide in about these issues.

The marriage happened with many red flags to suggest that I should have not done it. We were late at getting the license, the keys got locked in the car, and lastly, we did not have anyone there from either family to wish us well. I had my teammates stand in the wedding as witnesses, which they all told me I was crazy to be doing this, and they were right. We got a hotel room, partied all night, and slept most of the next day away. Within forty-eight hours later, my new bride was off to a foreign country, and there I was all alone again. But this time, I had to make sure I took care of her.

Two days after she left, I got a call from the Red Cross telling me that my grandma had died. I did not know what to do. I got on a plane back to North Carolina, not knowing what to expect other than the family drama that always came with funerals. Sitting on the plane, I thought to myself about how I was completely alone now. While I had never been the best at communicating with the social construct of family, now if really felt as though I had no family. The only person that had care for me in any way that I would have called a parent was gone.

When I arrived at the house, there were a lot of people sitting around and talking, and some crying. As I made my way back to a room in the house, I heard people talking about me and wondering how I was going to act. They had no idea what I had seen since I left home. I got something to eat and found my usual place to hide in the house. Right in plain sight, because I was invisible to them, until they needed something from me, or something done that no one else would do.

I was only there for a day before the funeral, so trying to process everything around me was difficult. I did not get to say goodbye to her, and I knew that she had been sick for a while. When I arrived at the church, as with most black family funerals in my experience, this is where the drama began. The show of emotions, whether real or for show, was always over the top. I stood in front of the casket and looked at her. She was at peace. I felt tears rolling down my face; I made no sound. After what felt like an hour, I stepped a little closer to say goodbye, at which time I slipped one of my Air Force Good Conduct medals in her coffin.

I made sure no one saw it; this was for her, to let her know that I had been a good boy and to thank her for everything she had done for me. I stood in the back of the church and watched the drama unfold. Her youngest daughter was standing in front of the casket and started to cry and scream. She began to lose herself, and I went and picked her up and carried her out of the church. While small in stature, I was very strong, and the people watched as I walked by with her in my arms.

After the service, we were back at the house, that was now packed with people from all of the community. I again found my space and faded into the night air, watching and listening to the conversations around me. My biological mothers were in the house and being consoled by others. At one point, I looked across the room at her and wondered if she was every going to my way. While that never occurred, because she was focused on her other two sons and making sure they were OK and that everyone saw how much of a loving mother she was to them.

The next morning, I packed my things and asked my cousin, who was a year older than me, to drive me to the airport. As we drive, those sixty miles seem like a thousand. I looked out of the window, thinking this would be the last time I would ever see this place again. There was nothing left for me to here, and I was never coming back. My cousin asked me if I was OK, and I said yes. He and I had once been close growing up; however, we drifted apart because he was always treated like he was older and accepted by the men. I was treated like a little child and excluded from most of the things happening within the family.

When we arrived at the airport, I told him to take care and thanks for the ride. We shook hands, and I walked away and never looked back. When the plane took off and I felt the wheels leave the ground, all of the emotions came rushing out of my mind and body. I turned and looked out the window as tears rolled down my face, saying silently, I love you, grandma, goodbye, and thanks. As the clouds became thicker, I laid my head against the window and drifted off into a space of the unknown.

When I arrived back at my base, a friend picked me up from the airport. As we drove back, I told him to stop at the store so I could get something to drink. I picked up a 12-pack of beer and some gin. When I got back to my barracks, I locked the door, turned on some music, and drank the day away. I had three days before I had to go to work, so I drank for three days not talking to anyone. I had forgotten that I had gotten married, as well as I was about to be stationed overseas in a couple of months.

I shut down emotionally from everything around me. While I was able to perform my duties, I was not able to have any type of relationship. I found myself living in a place of darkness while there was so much going on around me. While I was functioning within a space that everyone around me thought I was fine and showed no concerns. Inside, I was eroding away from the feeling of abandonment and shame. I had mastered the ability to hide my emotions during my childhood that at this age, I was perfecting it without even knowing I was doing it.

I would party every day, laugh like no tomorrow and tell women what they wanted to hear to get what I needed. The day of survival was upon me, and I was not going to fall short regardless of the price. I finally got overseas with my spouse, whom I had only known for two months prior to getting married. I had not seen her for almost 4 months because she left the day after we got married for this duty station. So, this was the first day of actually being together as a married couple.

The military was great; they gave us a house to live in, and we bought things we needed, and the pretending continued. Both young and not knowing what life was about, we treated it as we were young roommates. We both have already committed adultery in this marriage, and the relationship was just a façade; however, we would not admit it. Our childhoods were similar to the point that neither one of us would accept failure in this relationship. So, we put the tools that we had obtained from the military to use. We adapted and tried to overcome all of the things that had occurred in the short time of being married.

Within the first three months of being in this country, I was pulled away for a special assignment because of a police action, as the government termed it. I left home on December 19 and returned on February 23 the following year. During this time, I saw things that no young twenty-year-old should have seen. But this was the military, so I had to grow up quickly and embrace the things around me. While the images were unforgettable, I had unknowingly trained myself to compartmentalize the events that were happening around me. This would become more dangerous to me as my life journey continued.

When I returned home to base housing, where I had left my spouse for more than three months, she looked at me as though I was a different person. I came back to a house with a dog and many new things. We never spoke about the things I had seen or done during my time away. It was like starting all over again. We remained in the country for another six months, then were relocated back to the states.

While we were happy to be leaving, it was also the beginning of the downfall of the marriage. We arrived at our new base in Nevada, and life changes and drama was nothing that I could have predicted. We worked in different areas, and the distance began to grow between us. I was lost in the darkness of losing the only person that I knew cared about me while trying to restart a marriage that was not built on love, but a necessity. We discovered that we were very different and that our paths were not align.

We did not have anyone to go to for guidance, so we remain together, despite the separation that continued to grow. It was like neither one of us wanted to be alone anymore. Her family was connected a little better, but not a secure structure that could have helped us become one. I had found out that her mother did not want her to be married to someone out of her race. So, did she marry me to spite her mother, did I marry her to not be alone? Either way, we both had ended up in the place we were trying to avoid.

This marriage was doomed, but we would not concede it to anyone. I had become a master at making things seem like something else, and this was no different than what had created my foundation of life. We played the game well, and everyone thought we were a great couple. After being in Nevada for two years, she got out of the military and began to work in the civilian sector. I remained in the military, and this gave both of us a safe place to become ourselves. I began to withdraw and drink more as the day's past.

I found myself asking for assignments to get away; I had placed myself back into the mindset of running and never stopping. The fall was near, and things were getting bad in the house. All I could do was think about my grandma, drink, and think about the fact that she had cheated on me. I was no saint; I acted out once I knew this had happened, but I never admitted it to her. This was the moment of truth; we should have gotten a divorce and walked away.

Finally, I made the decision to get out of the military and become a cop. While in the academy, I realized that I had found something that I was very good at and was happy for a moment. Being a cop seemed to complete all the thing that I was missing as a man, a son, and an individual. I could help people, and people would respect me for what I had become. It had been a long time since I felt this way; the last time was when I put on the military uniform.

I was so disconnected from her that it did not matter what she did or what she was doing. I began to live a separate life while living in the same house with her. The second thing I mastered as an unwanted child. I had to pretend that the space I was in had walls which only I could see and hide behind. This was my security from the real world around me. I had everyone in the community thinking I was a great guy and husband. I was a great cop, and I out worked all the guys in my area. I knew how to build relationships with people and gain their trust.

It was near the end of winter, right after my wife's birthday, when my wife told me we were going to have a baby. My first response was, "Is it mine?" She got mad and left. I did not know how to receive this information. When she came back, I apologized and stated this would be our new beginning. We talked all night, and things were better in the morning. We told our friends, and everyone was happy for us, except for our families.

As the time passed with the pregnancy, I began to think about what kind of father I would or could be. I had no point of reference in my life; my father had disowned me even before I was born. My references for what a father was, was not positive; drinking, cheating, and fighting were all I had even seen. I told myself that I would be the father that I always wanted when my child was born. It did not matter if it was a boy or girl; I just wanted a healthy child to love.

Again, I did not know how to love, neither give nor receive love. So, I began to doubt myself again. As the time came close to our child being born, I was trying to emulate the positive things I saw others doing with their spouses and in their homes. We bought everything she wanted for the baby. I talked to a realtor about a house because I did not want to bring my baby home to a place I was not proud of. Living in a small town, there were not a lot of choices for great homes. I wanted the best for my child; I wanted him/her to be proud to come home and bring their friends to our home.

Chapter 8

From the moment I brought my child home, the world changed. I made a promise to myself that I would be the best father I could. I would provide my child with everything and more. My child was born the day before Thanksgiving in 1994. The first night home, I sat up looking at her while my wife was sleeping. I could not sleep, as I looked at her, my mind was flooded with thoughts of how I was left alone in a room as I was told by those who were supposed to have love me. Lying in a shoe box like an old pair of shoes, small enough to be forgotten about.

I remembered the stories of how everyone would look at me as if I was not going to survive, as I slept in the drawer of a dresser. I could not understand why these things were running through my mind at this time. I was looking at the most precious gift a person could have in their life. However, I finally realized that I was not a gift to anyone when I arrived. I was treated like a package left on the steps of the house, and it would be placed in the closet, forgotten that it had arrived.

I started to cry as I sat in the dark, looking at my beautiful child. I got angry, shaking and could not breathe. I laid down next to her and closed my eyes so I could hear her breath and her heartbeat. I was lost and in pain, happy yet sad, and the doubt began to set into my brain about not being able to be the father that she deserved. For the next couple of weeks, I kept fighting these thoughts without talking to anyone. As friends came to see our beautiful child, they laugh, and gave us hugs, and smiles were flowing like water from the faucet.

I sat and watched as my wife smiled and shared the laughter of other mothers. She seemed to be in the best space she had been since our marriage began. I went back to work and found myself focusing on the dark side of society once again. I lost my focus on the family and the promise of being something that I could never achieve. We moved into a new house that gave my wife and child everything they could want. I began to play the role that society had developed for me. Driven to create a facade of happiness while surrounded by material things that had no value to me. I was drinking so much that I could not remember how to feel without alcohol. Having the greatest moment of becoming a father also created the greatest fear of being a failure and worthless at the same time.

This darkness had consumed me in many ways that I never imagined. I found myself battling many demons, and the battles became more difficult. While I did not share the loss of two good friends in the line of duty within a twelve-month time period, one prior to the birth of my child and the other just a few months after. I began to build walls within my mind to shield me from any more pain. This increased the space between my wife and me, but it did not matter to me. I was feeling like I was on an island alone, while surrounded by people every day.

I became so disconnected from my marriage that I began to have an emotional affair with another woman. At the time, I did not understand what that meant, nor did I care. I just wanted someone to talk to without feeling like I was being judged by every word or by how I looked. This caused more trouble within the house and on my job to the point that my wife used her father's health to move back to the place where she grew up. Taking my daughter away from me was not an option in my mind or heart.

I walked away from the only job other than the military that I had wanted more and never looked back. After packing up the house and driving east to follow the only person who gave me a reason to continue to try and do what is right, I found myself holding my daughter in the darkness once again while everyone was sleeping. I was now in a place where I had never been, surrounded by people who did not want me in their lives. While so sad, it was so familiar that I told myself I could survive this again to be with my daughter. Putting everything behind me, I pushed forward and found myself working once again in uniform and chasing ghost. This time, I told myself that I would invest in myself to ensure I would never have to feel like I was worthless again. I started college and worked at the same time. This was challenging because my wife did not want to work, and I did not want my child in daycare.

So, we agreed that I would take care of the family until our child was in school. I worked two jobs and went to school. For more than two years, I worked seven days a week while going to school to make sure they both had what they needed and more. My wife was living near her family, and she wanted to show them that she had made it with her life, so the façade became bigger. We were living way beyond our means, and I was working to keep up the image. I keep a smile on my face, so everyone thought that things were good between us and the family life was perfect just as she displayed it.

Just with any veneer, it begins to fade. When our daughter started school, I supported my wife in her goals of getting her education as well. She was attending college while our child was in school and was at home with her. I continued to work the two jobs and go to school. Time was not on my side when it came to enjoyment. I felt drained but wanted to make sure I was able to provide for my family at the same time. Losing focus on the marriage while focusing on what I thought was important gave me the drive to continue.

As I began to embrace my education, I found myself wondering who I was and if I had the skills to become anything more. I watched and listened to the others around me about their dream jobs and the places that they grew up in. Many of them talked about their families, and some even asked about mine. When I was asked about my parents, I had to think for a moment about what I would say or what they would accept. I did not want anyone to feel pity for me; I did not want to be looked down on as the bastard child once again in my life. I remembered what I had put in my file in the military, that my parents were unknown, and I was raised by my grandma.

This was the story that had become my truth about the family that did not exist. Most people appeared to accept it and left things alone, while some continued to make me feel less than in their own way. While I was not the best student,

I enjoyed reading and drifting off to pretend that I could be something someday. I was almost thirty years old now, with a child who I wanted nothing more than to ensure she had a world where people would see her for who she was and accept her in her space and place.

The summer was ending, and the new school year was starting. I was working a third shift at one job and a day shift at the other. Going to school three days a week and sleeping about three hours a day. The world as I knew it was shattered once again. I came home from work to find my wife and child all packed up and leaving to go west. I did not understand what was going on with my wife. While her father had died and I knew she was struggling with things, seeing her run was like looking into the mirror and seeing myself.

I did not try to stop her as she drove away. I sat in the darkness alone, wondering what to do next. I knew what I had to do, but for the first time in a long time, I felt as though I was finding myself through school and did not want to run any more. However, the one promise that I had never broken was to always be there for my daughter. So, within a couple of months, I packed up everything and moved once again. People had started talking about me, which was nothing new in my world. They would make comments about how you could just drop your life and move. My only response each time was that I would never leave my baby girl.

They would stop and then just say, *OK, I get it.* But they did not get it; my daughter was the only thing in the world that was keeping my heart alive. I had nothing else to motivate me to do anything in my life. Once I arrived in a city called Phoenix, we settled down and I went to work as usual, in uniform and hiding in the shadows of myself again. This time we built a house in hopes that we would stay here forever and allow our daughter to grow up, find happiness within herself, and make friends. I enrolled in college and encouraged my wife to do the same so that we could afford the things she wanted out of life.

We worked hard, and after two years, we were graduating from college. It appears things were finally going to change, and that maybe we would make it after all. The house was great, and our daughter was smiling and making friends. Until my demons began to reappear within my mind, and this time it was a war. I fought off the drinking, which led to me talking to another woman, which led to fighting, which brought back the drinking. Suddenly, it was like reliving the same dream all over, and this time we were headed for a divorce.

When the paperwork was filed, my wife decided she was moving back to her home and taking our daughter with her. Again, while she had not dealt with her own demons, she was willing to go back to the place that she called home. I stooped the divorce process, sold the house, and moved back with her. This time, I knew in my mind that the only reason I was here was to be with my daughter; it did not matter what happened in the marriage. I was not going to abandon my daughter. I never wanted her to feel the way I felt about my biological parents.

While this journey was only in the middle, this was a short stop. My wife lasted two years before she picked up and moved my daughter to North Carolina. She stated she needed to grow up and know the other side of her heritage.

I got mad and told her not to do this; she did not understand what she was doing to our daughter. She did not care; she had met some of the family and thought it would be great to live near them. But her demons were driving her away from what she knew as a family.

67

Chapter 9

I felt like I had just arrived in hell when we stopped in North Carolina. I told her I did not want to live anywhere near my family. I got a job in a city about two hours away. For my family to come see me there was like it was twenty hours away; I knew they would never come. We settled down, and for the first couple of weeks, I withdrew from everyone and everything. I did not know how to feel living there because I had promised to never return after my grandma had passed away. How much more could I sacrifice for my daughter? How much did I have left in me to mask the scars and pain, knowing that they would act as if nothing had ever happened and that I was treated like all of the other kids?

I was waiting for the phone call and to hear someone say, "Why are you acting so ungrateful?" I was told several times that I needed to come care of my biological mother because it was my job. After being gone for more than twenty-three years, nothing had changed about the way I was seen or treated. I was to be grateful to a person who did not want me in her life. A woman who left her child behind like a hat or pair of shoes and just stated someone will used them I got others. The elders of the family tried to make me feel like I was disrespectful, and as her oldest son, I was my responsibility to take care of her.

This just drove a wedge deeper within my mind and heart. I was not going to give what little energy left in me to someone who did not care about what happened to me. My biological mother had poisoned me with the hate and disgust she fed me for almost nine months. Leaving me undernourished, underdeveloped, and undesirable to anyone who wanted a child. This time, I focused on myself. I made sure my daughter had what she needed, and I worked on finding myself. I left my wife to find herself, knowing that the marriage was going to end the moment my daughter was done with high school.

For the next five years, I lived two lives. One was in the space with my daughter, and the other was within the space of my head. I never let anyone get close to me, which in turned I was pushing my daughter away emotionally and did not know it. I watched as my daughter struggled in finding herself, and I tried to support her the best I could. I knew in my heart that she was lost, and I did not take the time to help her through the darkness.

After four years in North Carolina, I could not take it anymore; I was drained and wanted out. I knew that if I could just get away and file for divorce, then maybe I had a chance to survive. But I could not leave my daughter, so I took her with me. I left with the plan of filing for divorce when we got settled. I had found a job, and everything was set for me to leave. We had only been gone for two months before my wife showed up and wanted to try and work things out. This was her way of coming between my daughter and me. I did not fight her being with us because of our daughter, so for the last time, the cycle continued.

I was working and going to school, this time for a master's degree. I wanted to make sure I could have the life I thought I deserved and give something to my daughter because of me not being there for her when she needed me the most. Both of us were working in good jobs, and the façade was back in place. However, so were the demons. This time I did not fight them at all; I let them manifest themselves in whatever way they came out.

As time drew closer to our daughter graduating from high school, so did the moment of getting the divorce. This time it was nothing to stop me from completing this task. My wife knew what was coming, so she put her plan in place with the help of the one person that she once ran from, her mother. When the divorce was filed four months before the graduation date, she showed her cards while waiting for everything. She had quit her job two years before the divorce so that she could be paid alimony. This was her way of making sure I could not afford to live the way I had planned.

When this happened, I moved out and got my own place. Regardless of what I had to pay, I was not going to allow a decision made twenty years earlier to define the next twenty years of my life. Things were very hard for me; I was alone in the dark, my relationship with my child was destroyed, and I felt myself slipping back into the world of alcohol to cope. I kept my head above water by using the sense of failure as the life preserve that I needed. The feeling of abandonment was flooding over me every day, and it got stronger as time passed.

I focused my energy on the job, which made me keep a smile on my face to be successful. Meanwhile, I lost myself in meaningless relationships to fulfill my physical needs. As this was something that I had mastered and was able to do without emotional attachment, even though I gave the perception of being attached. I reverted to my old ways after my grandma's death to survive what felt like the death of me when my child did not want anything to do with me.

After about a year, I began to evaluate my life, and I needed to find direction and a purpose to move forward. I was looking through a box and found a note that I had made some two decades before. On this paper was a list of things that I wanted to accomplish to make my grandma proud of me. I had accomplished most of them, but one stood out to me, and at that moment, I knew what I needed to get myself out of this hole.

I contacted a recruiter and reenlisted back into the military. I needed something to hold me accountable for the things I was going to do with my life. The military was the only place that had given me a purpose and structure where I felt I could accomplish anything. I completed all of the requirements and took the oath. When I left the office, driving back to my apartment, I felt like it was a repeat from the first time. I did not tell anyone what I had done; I did not let anyone know about me being back in the military until about 8 months after the fact. I had to tell my employer so that I could get the time off that I needed; however, I lived in a bubble and worked on getting myself out of the hole that I had allowed myself to fall into.

Chapter 10

Things were going great, and for the first time in almost two years, I felt like I had a purpose again. While I had not spoken to my child in two years, I knew where I was going for myself. The feeling of abandonment was starting to fade away, but mostly I had replaced it with the attachment of the military. I focused on the long game of getting my retirement and feeling like I had accomplished something in my life. The uniform became my new life vest, and I was going to be proud of what I could accomplish in the next decade.

I met someone, and this time I told myself I was going to be as open and honest as I knew how. I did not want to be alone anymore; I wanted to love someone and to feel love, real love this time. We started out slow, and I enjoyed the walks and talks with her. She was divorced and had children, so I did not want rush things. Just as we started to spend time together, I got orders to be deployed for a year. Again, another flashback; what was going to happen once I was gone? I thought about being cheated on life my ex-wife had done. I thought about being abandoned by her because she would not wait for me to return.

I placed all these negative thoughts in my head, which started me down a path of doubt about myself again. But this time I took a different approach. I talked to her about all of this, and we worked out a plan to make things work. She was so supportive that I did not know how to accept it or trust it at the same time. As the time got near for me to leave, I told her that I would trust in her and that we would work through this and continue to grow together.

When I got on the plane, I sat there as if I was the eighteen-year-old running away from the pain that I had endured all my life. My brain was flooded with emotions and flash backs to the feeling of emptiness and being alone. As the darkness appeared out the window, I felt my heart close off, and my view became the sight of a tunnel with no light in the distance. I was surrounded by hundreds of people but felt as though I was the only soul on board the airplane. I felt like the blood running through my veins was toxic poison, and there was nothing I could do about it.

We landed, and for the next year, I lived like I was lost within myself. I put on the façade that I knew would work around anyone at any time. Again, I worked like a charm, and I was successful in the things that were given to me. I had people coming to me for advice and wanting to be near me for support. However, I was being drained of the energy that I needed to sustain the charade. I could not let anyone know that I was a hollow shell of a man who could not help himself at this point. I would fight the demons every day to survive and stay as true to the things I wanted moving forward in my life.

While this duty gave me sort of a safe place to help me with the demons, it also presented others that I thought was no longer an issue. I fought these demons one day at a time and took the energy that I had and put it into my physical wellbeing. Doing this left me little energy to give to the demons which kept my mind occupied otherwise. I was allowed to take some time off and meet my girlfriend for a cruise. This came at the right moment because I was holding on by a thread.

We had a blast and reconnected, talked, and enjoyed the time together. She also needed this as well to ensure she had made the right choice for her as well. We talked about everything that had happened since I left. We laughed and enjoyed each day, looking forward. This was just what I needed to help me overcome the demons within me. She went back home, and I went back to my assignment. The time seemed to fly by, and soon it was time to return home. The moment came to get on the plane, and my heart was racing. When I felt the wheels come off the ground, my mind began to run through every old file it could find to prepare myself for what I could potentially be coming home to. The demons were revived, and the sadness of abandonment began to fill my thoughts. While my girlfriend had given me no reason to think this way, it was the experiences that had led me to the nightmare within my mind.

Prior to this, I had never come home to a positive environment. There was always drama, and someone or everyone made me feel as though I was not worthy of an explanation or should be given one. I walked around on eggshells like I was a visitor within my own house. How could I stop this from happening within my mind? I was going back to my own space; there was no one there to judge me, nor did I have to answer to anyone when I arrived.

For the next several hours, I worked through all these thoughts. I remembered something that my counselor, Dr. Britton, had once told me in a session. Oh, maybe I forgot to let you know. I was also being treated for PTSD and depression. Dr. Britton was the best thing that ever happened to me after the divorce. Working with him helped me get back into the military and get my life on track.

What Dr. Britton had told me was to take it one day at a time, and for me, it was important to live in the moment and not in the past. My mind was anticipating everything that could possibly happen, which caused me to overlook where I was now. My sense of abandonment left me in the mist of not trusting anyone to protect myself from getting hurt. This was the shield I created from childhood because of the environment I entered each time I walked into a place or space around the people who supposedly loved me. No one had ever waited for me; no one had ever cared for me in a manner that I was placed first. I had never experienced real love, nor did I know how to accept it when it was offered.

I understood how it felt not to be wanted or less than others, even invisible to those standing next to me. These were the only feelings I knew existed in my world. As the plane traveled through the night sky, I cried in the darkness, silently. I wanted more than ever to finally know what it felt like to come home to someone who really loved me for me. With my eyes closed, I imagine her standing there, waiting to see me walk off the plane, and she would run to me and give me a hug.

The moment of truth came not soon after this, and it happened; she was there, and she did embrace me just like I had imagined. From that moment on, I knew I had to let go of the past and take a chance on a real future with what most had experienced: real love.

76

Chapter 11

As I continue to work with Dr. Britton on accepting happiness into my life, the world seems to want me to stay in the darkness of abandonment. My fiancé and I have moved in together, and life is going great until the latest in the Supreme Court decision regarding Roe v. Wade. This book is not about politics; it's about the abandonment of a child, me. So how did this action of a court cause me to slip back down the hole of darkness?

I began to imagine my child being forced to bring a child into this world because someone else's moral compass would not allow my child to decide for themselves. I was fed hatred, sadness, and anger as nourishment from an individual who did not want me, nor loved me. This individual was embarrassed and pressured by those around her to give birth to a child she did not want. At the time of my birth, society placed shame on a bastard child because of religion and the societal stigmatism associated with unwedded pregnancy.

This book is not a political-driven viewpoint, so please don't get lost in your agenda during this reflection. I wanted to ensure that there were some points of reference for those readers who may be thinking, "I would take a child into my home and love them as if they were my own." Maybe that is true for a small portion of those who do. However, on average, there are more than half a million children in foster care in the United States.

On average, there are about one hundred and thirty-five thousand adoptions in the United States. What happens to the three hundred and sixty-five thousand left to find for themselves in a society that will always look down on them because of the stigmatism of not being wanted? While I had a roof over my head and what would have been considered a safe place, the feeling of not being wanted by the individuals that brought you into this world makes everything seems harmful.

If an individual chooses to bring a child into this world, that person should create a space in which the child will not be reviewed as an object, or thing, or an even more damaging a burden in their life. Those individuals that were supposed to love me and treat me with kindness, I believe, did not know what that meant for themselves, let alone the ability to give it to an unwanted child. The development of a child is critical in the first five years of its life. Imagine hearing words like "somebody better take care of that boy" or "lord, that poor child is lucky to be alive."

To be fed negativity from the womb and throughout your environment as a child creates a coding within an individual that is hard to remove. Like getting mud on your shirt, just because you washed it does not mean the elements of the dirty are not there. I watched, listened, and felt the disdain individuals had toward me. The emotional rollercoaster dropped deep into my psychological and physiological pathways with many twists and turns.

Going through counseling was the most demanding thing that I have ever done in my life. While that is a bold statement, given the fact that I have been through two wars and several conflicts as a Soldier. But there is no greater battle than the one within yourself to accept yourself for who you are. I must begin to let go of all those negative things within my mind and body that, at one point, I thought defined me. Then I had to begin building the things about who I am to redefine how I saw the individual in the mirror.

I still have days where I sit and cry when no one is around. I look out into the sky and wonder if I would ever get that moment, like most kids, where their father or mother would tell them how proud they are of them. However, I know that day will never come. For me, after more than five decades of emotional scares, I have finally begun to heal and allow myself to be happy.

This has come with a price that I wish I did not have to pay. The price of failed marriage, relationships, alcoholic issues, and many other things. But the costliest of them all was the damage to my own child for not being the father that I should have at the most critical time of their life.

So, to digress, the latest thing that is occurring within our society has caused the wound of abandonment to surface once more. As I work through this with my counselor, I wonder how many other children will be forced into an environment of unwantedness. How many would be left with the stigma of worthlessness or the unacceptance of others? How many thousands of unwanted souls will be scattered across the United States of America in hopes of the American Dream? In which that dream becomes a nightmare because of the individual being forced to bring them into their own nightmare of not having a choice.

The great debate will continue, and the religion, morale, and ethical opinions of the few will continue to place the burden of life upon the unwanted souls in our society. Which the cycle will continue, a child who is powerless to the environment which surrounds them will soak up the negative nourishment from an unloving mother. Who, by force, fed this soul what was reflected upon her?